Antonín
DVOŘÁK
CZECH SUITE
Op. 39 / B. 93
(1879)

Study Score
Partitur

PETRUCCI LIBRARY PRESS

ORCHESTRA

2 Flutes
2 Oboes
English horn
2 Clarinets
2 Bassoons

4 Horns
2 Trumpets

Timpani

Violins I
Violins II
Violas
Violoncellos
Double Basses

Duration: ca.23 minutes

First performance: May 16, 1879
Prague, Provisional Theatre
Provisional Theatre Orchestra / Adolf Cech

ISBN: 978-1-60874-177-9
This score is a slightly modified unabridged reprint of the score
issued in 1955 by the Czech state publisher SNKLHU, plate H. 519.
The score has been scaled to fit the present format.

Printed in the USA
First Printing: August, 2015

CZECH SUITE
Op. 39 / B.93

I. PRELUDIUM
(PASTORALE)

Antonín Dvořák (1841-1904)
Edited by Otakar Šourek

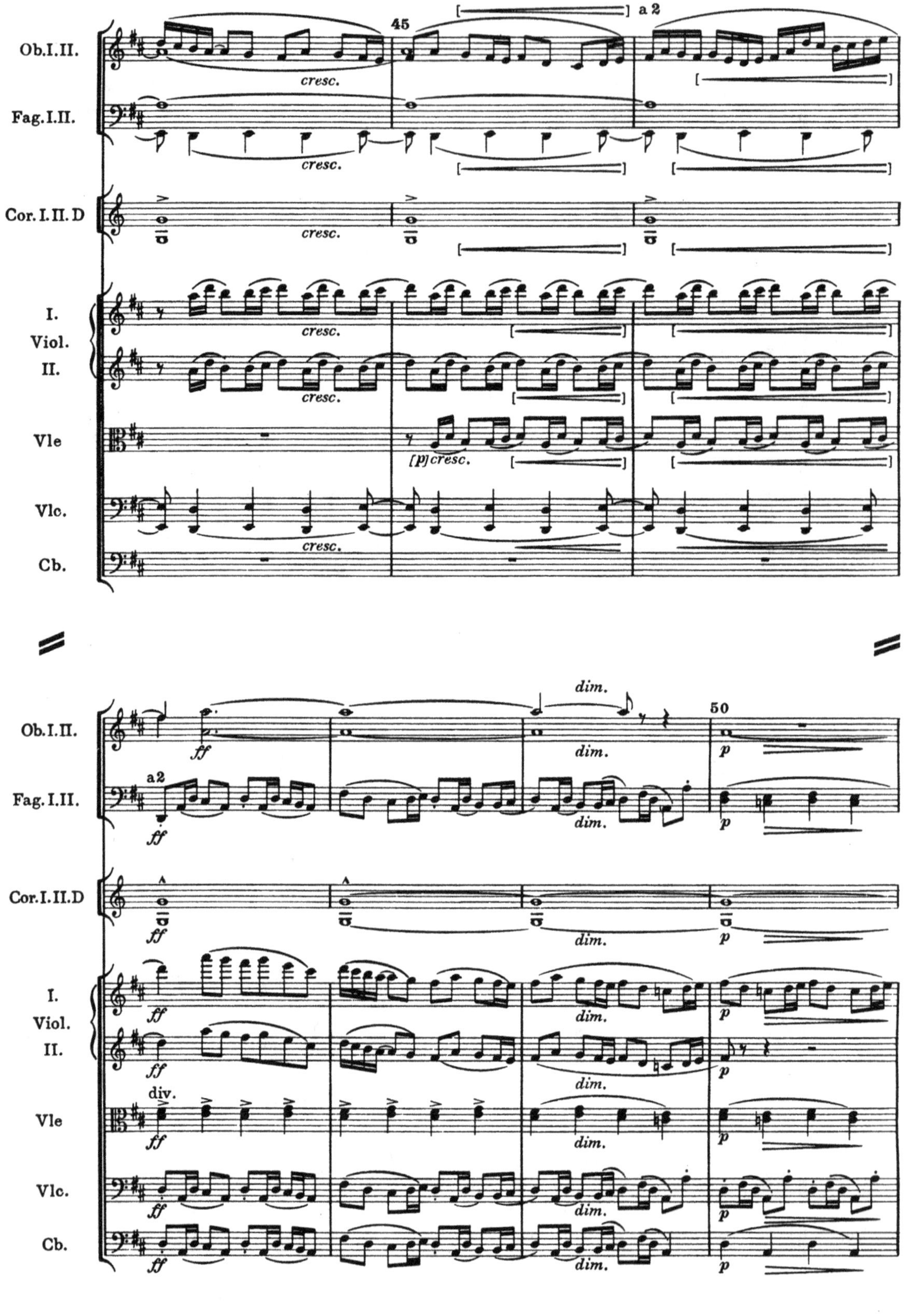
Ob.I.II.
Fag.I.II.
Cor.I.II.D
I.
Viol.
II.
Vle
Vlc.
Cb.
45
a 2
cresc.
[p] cresc.
div.
dim.
50
ff
p

II. POLKA

14

Polka D.C. sin al Fine

III. SOUSEDSKÁ
(MINUETTO)

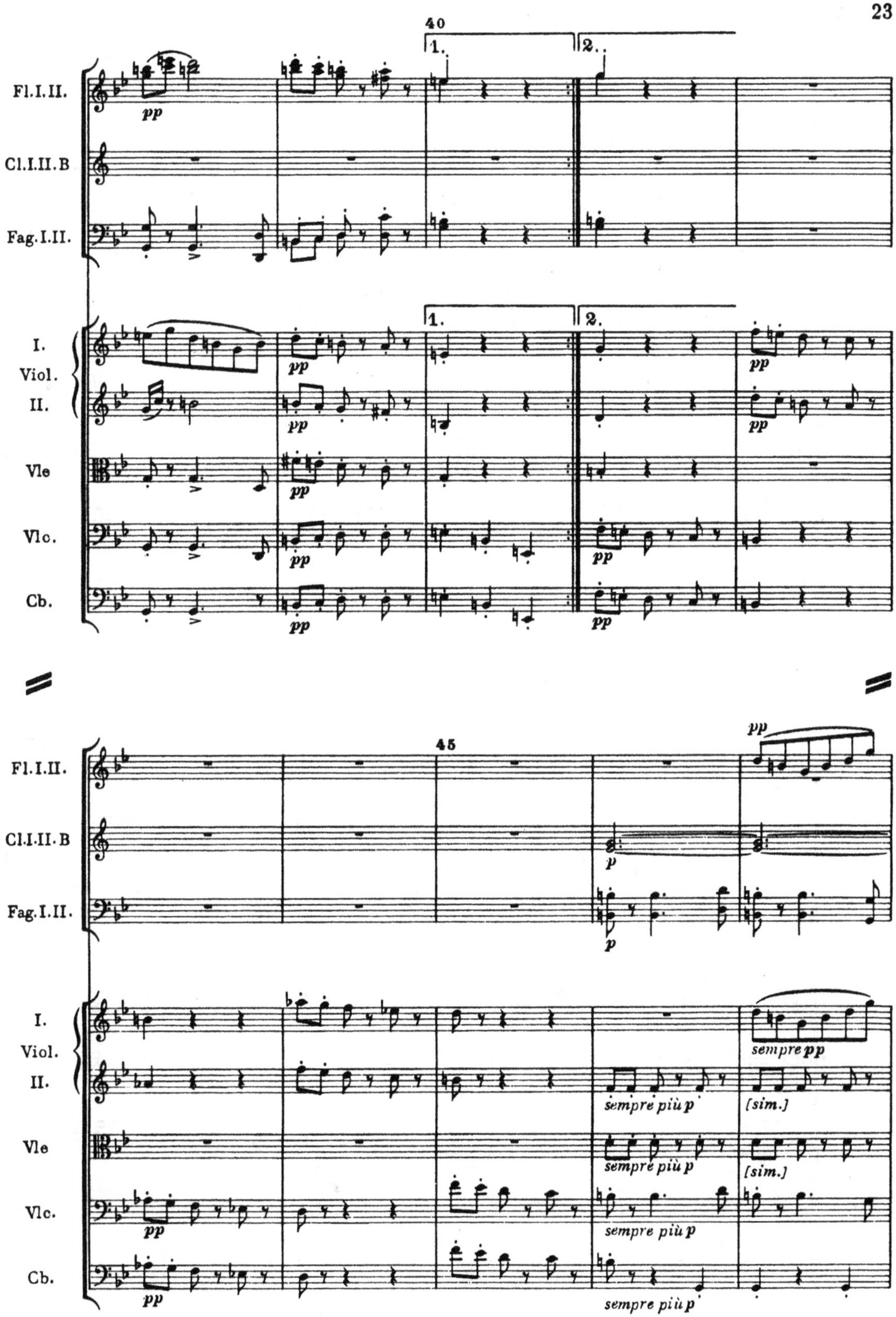
40
1.
2.
Fl.I.II.
Cl.I.II.B
Fag.I.II.
I.
Viol.
II.
Vle
Vlc.
Cb.
pp
45
p
sempre pp
sempre più p
[sim.]

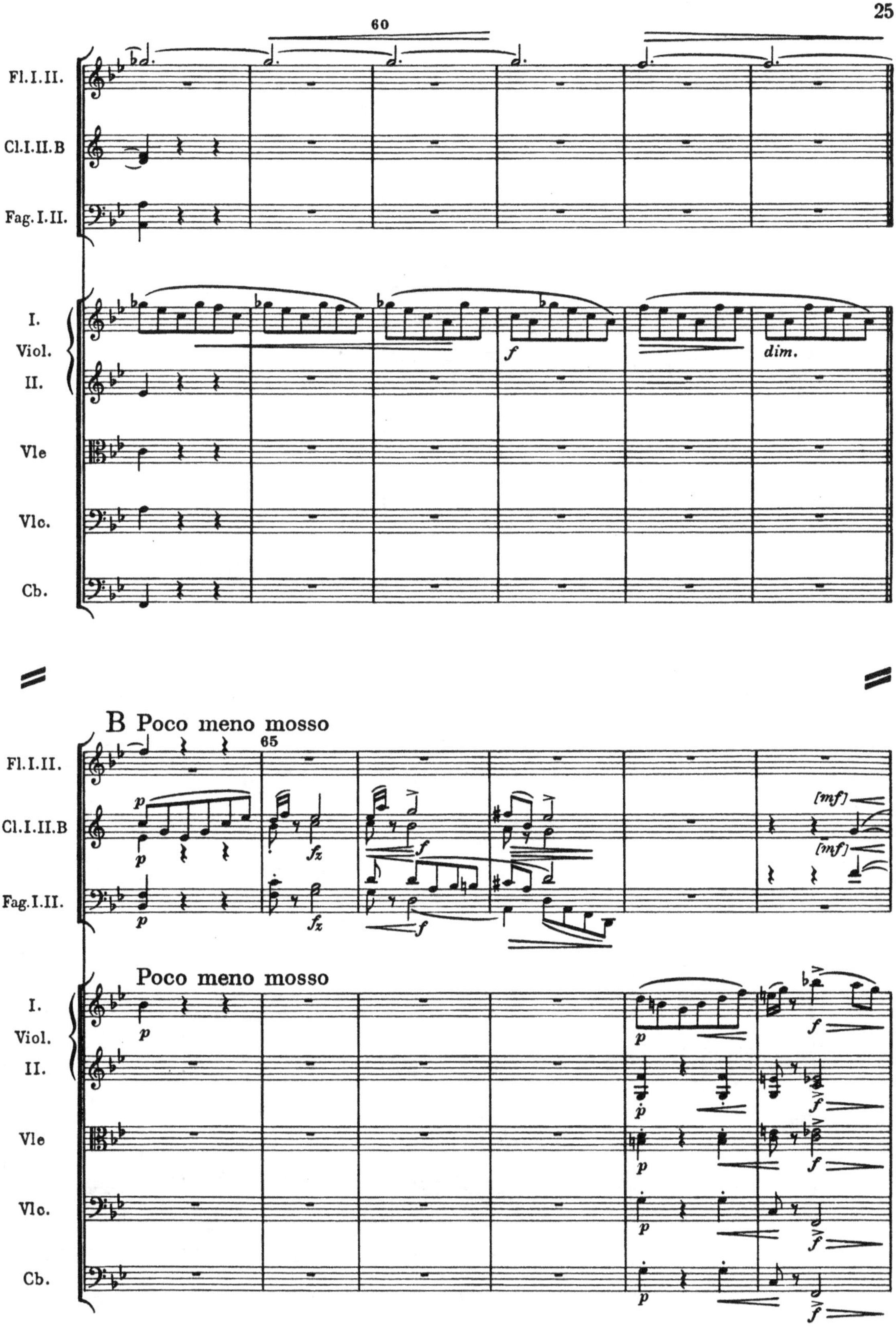
60
Fl.I.II.
Cl.I.II.B
Fag.I.II.
I.
Viol.
II.
Vle
Vlc.
Cb.
f
dim.
B Poco meno mosso
65
p
fz
f
[mf]
Poco meno mosso
p
f

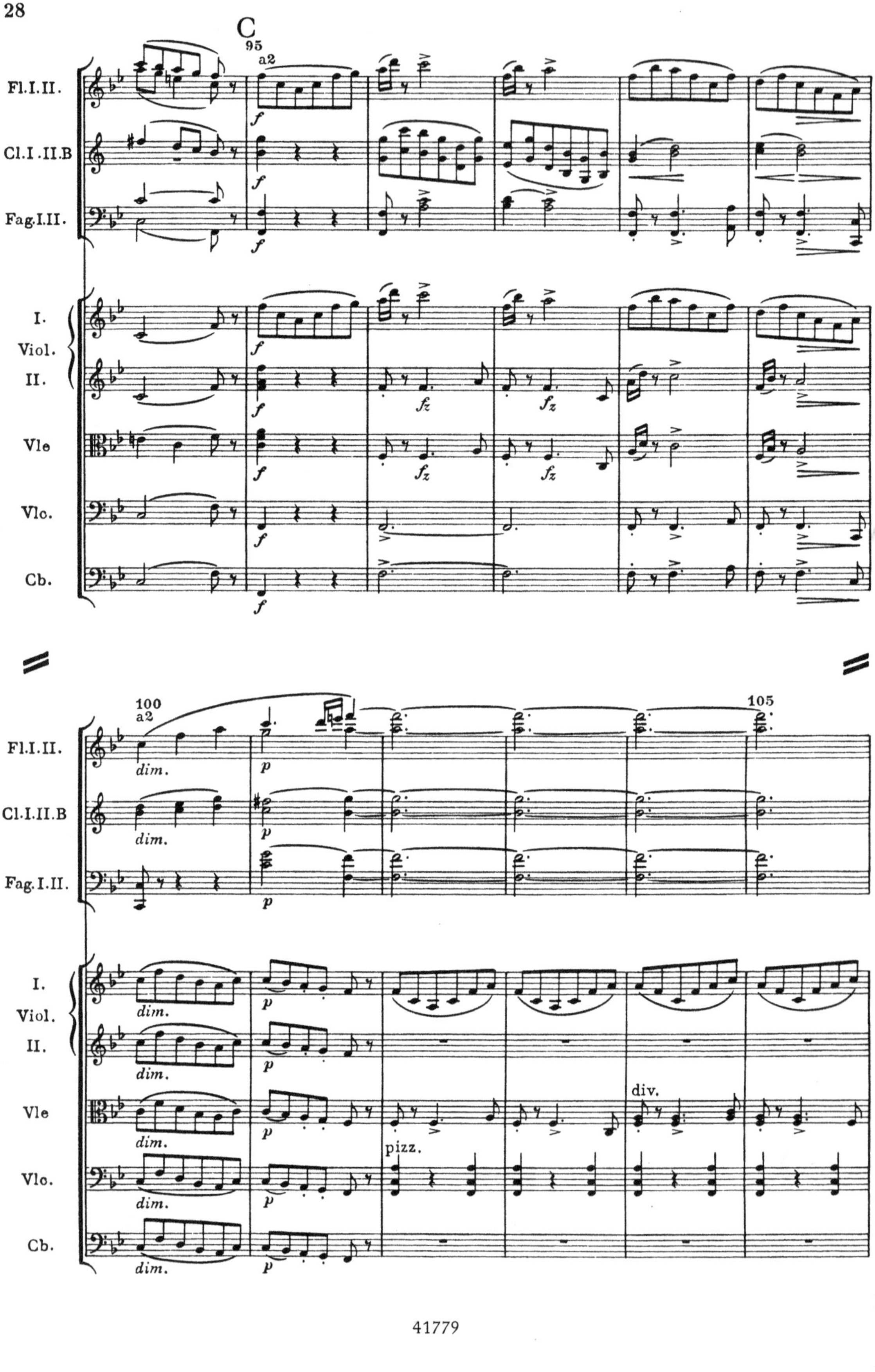
C
95
a2
Fl.I.II.
Cl.I.II.B
Fag.I.II.
I.
Viol.
II.
Vle
Vlo.
Cb.
f
fz
100
105
a2
dim.
p
div.
pizz.

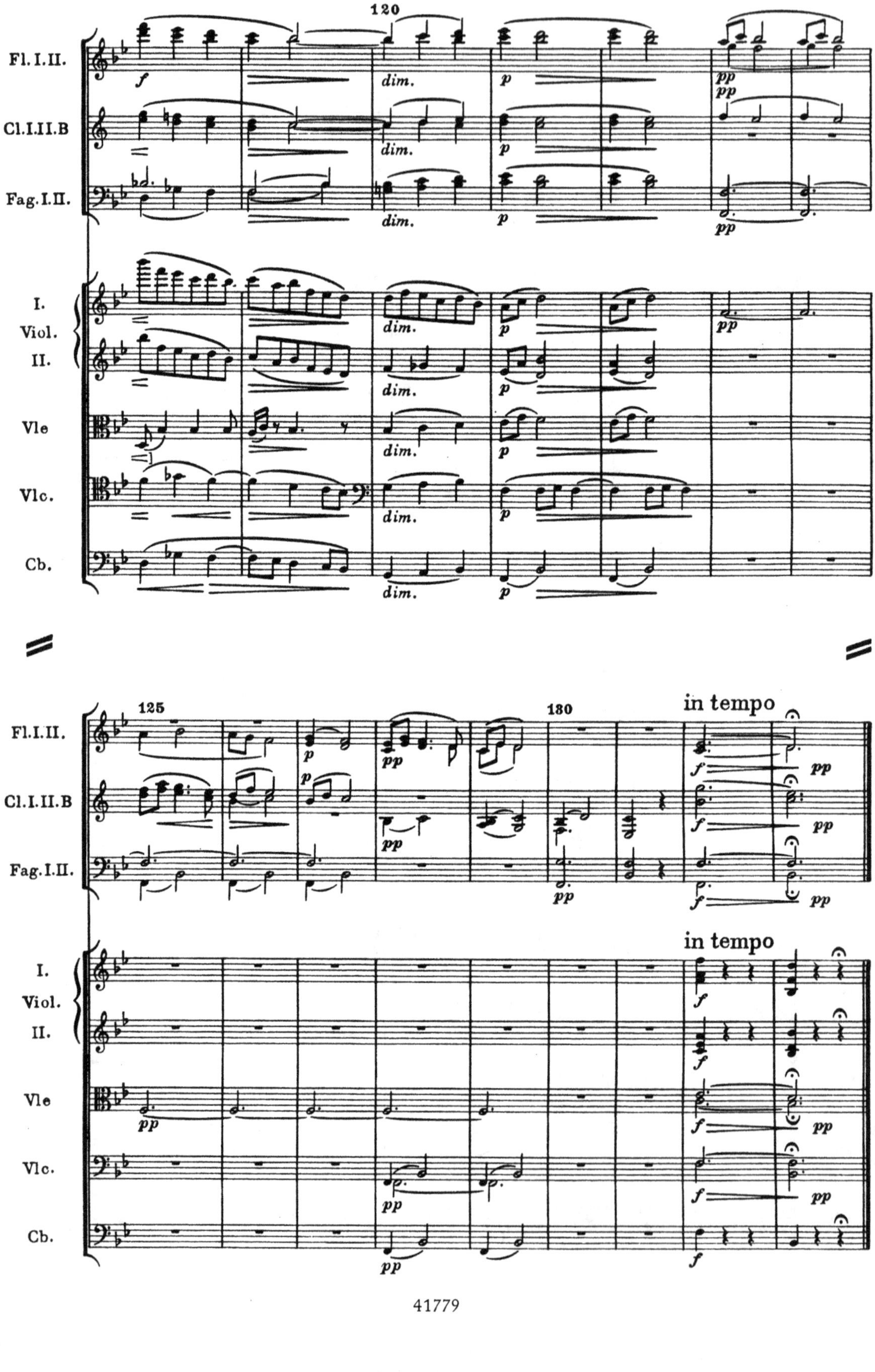
120
Fl. I. II.
Cl. I. II. B
Fag. I. II.
I.
Viol.
II.
Vle
Vlc.
Cb.
dim.
125
in tempo
in tempo

IV. ROMANCE
ROMANZA

*) Není-li anglický roh, budiž vzat roh basetový.
Ad lib. Corno *di bassetto.*

33

A

38

V. FINALE
(FURIANT)

44

52

64

www.ingramcontent.com/pod-product-compliance
Lightning Source LLC
Chambersburg PA
CBHW081349040426
42450CB00015B/3360